For Marie Ernestine Gorby – my partner and soul mate.
And for the many other teachers who have led me to
the Kingdom Within.

May these images speak to you wherever you are on life's journey.
May they open spiritual windows to God's kingdom
which is found within.
—Gary Gorby

Morehouse Church Supplies
A division of Church Publishing Incorporated

Copyright © 2011

Published by Morehouse Church Supplies, a division of Church Publishing Incorporated, 445 Fifth Avenue, New York, NY 10016, www.churchpublishing.org.

978-0-8192-2745-4

Living with the Psalms Journal

Recording Your Spiritual Journey

Photography by Gary Gorby

(resident of Twin Lakes)

They are like trees planted by streams of water, which yield their fruit in its season, and their leaves do not wither. In all that they do, they prosper. — Psalm 1:3

I cry aloud to the Lord, and he answers me
from his holy hill. — Psalm 3:4

O Lord, in the morning you hear my voice;
in the morning I plead my case to you,
and watch. — Psalm 5:3

O Lord, our Sovereign, how majestic
is your name in all the earth! — Psalm 8:9

O Lord my God, in you I take refuge; save me from all my pursuers, and deliver me. — Psalm 7:1

O Lord, our Sovereign, how majestic is your name in all the earth! You have set your glory above the heavens. — Psalm 8:1

You show me the path of life. In your presence there is fullness of joy; in your right hand are pleasures forevermore. — Psalm 16:11

Guard me as the apple of the eye; hide me in the shadow of your wings. — Psalm 17:8

The Lord is my rock, my fortress,
and my deliverer, my God, my rock in
whom I take refuge. — Psalm 18:2

*My God in his steadfast love
will meet me.* — Psalm 59:10a

*Lift up your heads, O gates! and be lifted up,
O ancient doors! that the King of glory
may come in.* — Psalm 24:7

To you, O Lord, I lift up my soul. — Psalm 25:1

From your lofty abode you water the mountains;
the earth is satisfied with the fruit of your work.
— Psalm 104:13

For he will hide me in his shelter in the day of trouble;
he will conceal me under the cover of his tent;
he will set me high on a rock. — Psalm 27:5

Make a joyful noise to the Lord, all the earth;
break forth into joyous song
and sing praises. — Psalm 98:4

*I will instruct you and teach you
the way you should go. — Psalm 32:8a*

As the deer longs for flowing streams,
so my soul longs for you, O God. — Psalm 42:1

Out of Zion, the perfection of beauty,
God shines forth. — Psalm 50:2

For God alone my soul waits in silence,
for my hope is from him. — Psalm 62:5

In his hand are the depths of the earth; the heights of the mountains are his also. — Psalm 95:4

Be still before the Lord and wait patiently for him.
— Psalm 37:7

It is you who light my lamp; the Lord, my God,
lights up my darkness. — Psalm 18:28

*Even though I walk through the darkest valley, I fear
no evil; for you are with me; your rod and your staff —
they comfort me.*   — *Psalm 23:4*

*I walk before the Lord in the
land of the living. — Psalm 116:9*

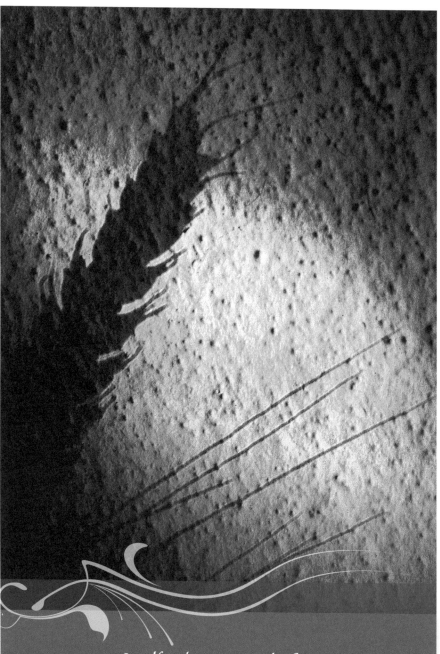

Steadfast love surrounds those
who trust in the Lord. — Psalm 32:10b

My soul waits for the Lord more than those who watch
for the morning, more than those who watch
for the morning. — Psalm 130:6

Be strong, and let your heart take courage,
all you who wait for the Lord. — Psalm 31:24

So teach us to count our days that we may
gain a wise heart. — *Psalm* 90:12

How great are your works, O Lord!
Your thoughts are very deep! — Psalm 92:5

Happy are those whose help is the God of Jacob,
whose hope is in the Lord their God. — Psalm 146:5

How weighty to me are your thoughts, O God!
How vast is the sum of them! — *Psalm* 139:17

The heavens proclaim his righteousness;
and all the peoples behold his glory. —Psalm 97:6

How lovely is your dwelling place,
O Lord of hosts! — Psalm 84:1

*In you, O Lord, I seek refuge; do not let me ever
be put to shame; in your righteousness deliver me.*
— *Psalm 31:1*

The Lord will give what is good, and our land
will yield its increase. — Psalm 85:12

Great are the works of the Lord, studied by
all who delight in them. — Psalm 111:2

When you send forth your spirit, they are created;
and you renew the face of the ground. — Psalm 104:30

"Come," my heart says, "seek his face!"
— Psalm 27:8

*I will sing of your steadfast love, O Lord,
forever; with my mouth I will proclaim your
faithfulness to all generations.* — Psalm 89:1

You are indeed my rock and my fortress; for your name's sake lead me and guide me. — Psalm 31:3

The earth has yielded its increase; God,
our God, has blessed us. — Psalm 67:6

Light dawns for the righteous, and joy
for the upright in heart. — Psalm 97:11

You visit the earth and water it,
you greatly enrich it. — Psalm 65:9a

*Our soul waits for the Lord; he is
our help and shield.* — Psalm 33:20

Let heaven and earth praise him, the seas and everything that moves in them. — *Psalm* 69:34

May you be blessed by the Lord, who made heaven and earth. — Psalm 115:15

Let them praise the name of the Lord, for he commanded and they were created. — Psalm 148:5

Let the favor of the Lord our God be upon us,
and prosper for us the work of our hands –
O prosper the work of our hands! — Psalm 90:17

*God will send forth his steadfast
love and faithfulness.* — Psalm 57:3b

Open to me the gates of righteousness,
that I may enter through them
and give thanks to the Lord. — Psalm 118:19

May the glory of the Lord endure forever;
may the Lord rejoice in his works. — Psalm 104:31

Praise the Lord! O give thanks to the Lord,
for he is good; for his steadfast love endures forever.
— Psalm 106:1

Author Biography

Gary Gorby has been an educator for over four decades. With students from high school through university, he has used photography as a tool to help them experience the wonders of God's creation.

Gary has earned degrees in natural science from Bethany College (WV), West Virginia University, and Vanderbilt University. He gives seminars and retreats to church and civic groups on meditation and stress management using photography and the Psalms. He is an active member of the Church of the Holy Comforter in Burlington, North Carolina where he lives with his wife and can be reached at tentmaker66@yahoo.com.